The Sex Education Dictionary

for Today's Teens
& Pre-Teens

Dr. Dean Hoch & Nancy Hoch

1990

LANDMARK PUBLISHING ❖ POCATELLO, IDAHO

READERS'
COMMENTS

"Why not arm young people with the knowledge and understanding of their bodies and reproductive processes? **The Sex Education Dictionary for Today's Teens & Pre-Teens** does just that. Why hasn't somebody thought of this before?"
Nancy Kleckner, Executive Editor
Growing Child/Growing Parent

"I think **The Sex Education Dictionary for Today's Teens & Pre-Teens** is an excellent idea and should be helpful not only to teenagers, but also to parents who are trying to explain the sexual facts of life to their children."
D. James Kennedy, Ph.D., Senior Minister,
Coral Ridge Presbyterian Church

"There has been a need for this type of dictionary. Children, parents, and teachers frequently are looking for one source to easily explain sexual terms. This book is that source."
Betty Holbrook, Public Librarian
Coordinator of Children's and Young Adult Services

"Every family needs a copy."
Leon Ames, Parent

"This book makes parenting easier, especially when you're not sure what to say and how to say it."
Carla Waldram, Parent

"A great book for classroom use."
Tom Dunlap, Public School Teacher

"We know one of the major contributing factors to sexually-related problems, especially among our young people, is ignorance of basic facts. This book will go far towards helping to overcome this negative reality."
Mike Milstein, Ed.D., Professor & Chair, College of Education
The University of New Mexico

"This dictionary is right on target."
Bart P. Billings, Ph.D.
Licensed Clinical Psychologist

"...An asset to any collection."
Terry Hyer
Young Adult Librarian

"TV, movies, school—all raise questions about sex. Now we can get answers without embarrassment and in a straightforward way."
Sandra Blanchard, Teenager

THE SEX EDUCATION DICTIONARY FOR TODAY'S TEENS & PRE-TEENS

Dr. Dean Hoch and Nancy Hoch

Illustrations by Camille H. Severe

Forewords by William A. Coop, Jr., M.D.
and
John Lackey, M.D.P.A.

Landmark Publishing
P.O. Box 776
Pocatello, Idaho 83204
208-233-0075

Hoch, Dr. Dean E. and Hoch, Nancy
   The sex education dictionary for today's teens & pre-teens

   ISBN 0–9624209–0–5

   89–063577

                    Landmark Publishing
                    P.O. Box 776
                    Pocatello, Idaho 83204
                    208-233-0075

Book design by Steve Medellin/Serephin Multimedia, Inc.

Manufactured in the United States of America
10 9 8 7 6 5 4 3 2 1

Printed in the United States of America

First Edition

Acknowledgements

❖

Our special thanks to the following people: Camille Severe for her creative work on the illustrations; our editors, Marsha Latimer and Mary Lou Tuffin for their sensitive and helpful suggestions; our book designer, Steve Medellin, for his patience and perseverance, as well as his enthusiasm for the project; Carol Cartaino of Collier Associates and former Editor-in-Chief of Writers' Digest Books for her help in the fledgling stages of the book; Betty Holbrook, Coordinator of Children's Services and Chris Ellis, Marcia Aldredge, and Chris Castro, reference librarians, at the Pocatello Public Library for their kind assistance; Janie and John Lackey, nurse and doctor, and husband and wife, for their professional input and their friendship; Bert Coop, our children's pediatrician for many years, Bud Gardner, writing instructor at American River College in Sacramento, for his ongoing inspiration; and to all the many people who have shown their enthusiastic support for this project.

Dedication

❖

*Dedicated to young people everywhere
and to the premise
that light and knowledge are
always preferable to
darkness and ignorance*

Table of Contents

❖

Foreword

❖

Young people have a natural interest in and curiosity about love, birth, and sex. In today's world they are bombarded with movies, videos, and music that portray all aspects of human sexual relationships. Given this situation, a strong need exists to help them deal with these topics in an open, intelligent way. They need quick and easy access to an understanding of correct words relating to human sexuality.

Many times, just knowing correct terminology can help decision-making skills. A young person feels more informed when he or she knows proper words and understands biological functions and concepts. Knowledge increases self-esteem and helps young people cope with the changes inherent during adolescence as well as with sexual pressures during the formative years.

Until now, teens and pre-teens have not had a book to turn to when questions arise as to the meanings of terms having to do with human reproduction and related topics. *The Sex Education Dictionary* fills this important need.

Parents and teachers, as well as young people, will find this a helpful book. It is an outstanding resource tool for providing accurate information on an important subject.

Facts are always best learned in an atmosphere of concern and consideration. This is especially true regarding the subject of sexuality. This book can play an important role in developing a trusting bond, especially between parents and children. It can also be a boon for teachers at varying grade levels. It is designed to facilitate learning, and it does much toward accomplishing this goal.

William A. Coop, Jr., M.D.
Pediatrics Department
Kaiser Permanente Medical Group
Sacramento, California

Foreword

❖

It was surprising and disturbing for me to learn that there has been no book written to date addressing definitions of sex and sexual functions for teens and pre-teens. This type of book is important for several reasons.

First of all, the slang terms used by many teenagers in relation to sexuality frequently have connotations of no social or moral responsibility or obligation towards sexual function or sexual matters. Secondly, as a practicing gynecologist, I never cease to be amazed at the lack of basic understanding among many pre-teens and teens about just what causes the female to become pregnant.

I am equally concerned, as are a majority of my colleagues, about the rapid increase in sexually-transmitted diseases, particularly AIDS and hepatitis B. It seems more than reasonable that a proper understanding of anatomical parts and sexual function could play a real preventive role in bringing the escalating STD epidemic under control.

J.M. Lackey, M.D.P.A.
Board Certified OB/GYN
Pocatello, Idaho

Preface
To: Parents and Teachers

❖

The subject of sex has no doubt generated more interest among human beings than any other; and it has probably also generated more confusion.

While doing research in our local library, we discovered that a dictionary of reproductive terms had never been published. We found dictionaries for young people on sports, auto racing, and various other subjects, but none dealing with birth and sex. Nor was anything of this nature listed in *Books in Print*.

After talking with librarians, parents, and teachers, we determined that a strong need existed for this kind of book. We researched applicable terminology and compiled over 300 terms. Definitions for these terms are written in plain language for both teens and pre-teens.

This is a practical and versatile book; it is a reference tool for parents, teachers, and young people; it is a classroom aid for sex education and health classes; it is a resource for parents answering difficult questions at home. When a child asks, "What does abortion mean?" a parent or teacher can respond, "Let's look it up in **The Sex Education Dictionary**." The child becomes familiar with using the book and with getting correct information on unfamiliar terms. Crossword puzzles, word searches, and quizzes have been added to the book to enhance learning. These reproducible learning aids are designed to be helpful in the home and classroom setting.

Working as educators in both public and private schools and in community settings, we understand children's needs. Our five sons have added to our knowledge of what young people want and need to know about sex and reproduction. This book fills an important need. Even adults who have read the text say, "I wish I'd had a book like that when I was growing up."

Educators, librarians, physicians, and young people have read the book and have offered their suggestions. We are grateful for their help.

Since language changes and words are constantly being added to our vocabulary, we know revisions in this first edition will need to be made. Suggestions for additions or improvement to the text may be sent to us at Landmark Publishing, P.O. Box 776, Pocatello, Idaho 83204.

Dr. Dean & Nancy Hoch

A Note About Slang Terms

❖

For several reasons, we have purposely chosen to include only a very few slang terms in this edition. First, our intent is to acquaint teens and pre-teens with correct terminology, such as a doctor would use in his office, and to encourage the use of these words. Secondly, many sexually-related slang terms change rapidly. Younger teens do not recognize some of the slang words older teens are formulating and vice versa. Thirdly, slang terms vary widely from one part of the country to another and among various sub-cultures. And lastly, if we were to include all the slang terms available, the book would become unwieldy in size. Another edition may include slang terms, if we find a demand exists.

The Sex Education Dictionary for Today's Teens & Pre-Teens

Introduction
For Today's Young Readers

❖

Growing up can and should be a wonderful experience. At times, however, the whole process gets confusing. Sometimes, it's even a bit frightening.

As a young person, you know that many changes take place both on the inside and on the outside of every boy and girl. This is just part of adolescing—or changing into a young adult. These changes are natural and normal. They are also exciting. The important thing is to take all these changes in stride. And the best way to do this is to learn what is happening—to be able to understand the words you hear when people talk about growing up and becoming adults and parents. It's also important to be able to express yourself properly when talking about these matters and when asking questions.

You have a wonderful body. Each girl has the potential of one day becoming a woman and a mother, each boy, a man and a father. All the body parts are uniquely designed for the many tasks they are meant to carry out in a lifetime. Knowing about yourself and your body is an important part of the process of becoming an adult.

This isn't always easy. People on TV and in the movies, and even other kids you know, often talk about people's bodies and reproduction with incorrect words. Sometimes these words are used in a gross, vulgar way. Because of this you might have a problem learning the correct words and terms. This can make you uncomfortable.

Joanie, a sixth-grade girl, had this problem. One day she was talking to a friend about how babies are born. Joanie's friend, Lisa, told her that a baby is made when an egg from the mother comes together with "spam" from the father. From that day on, each time Joanie's mother served "Spam" for lunch, Joanie remembered her conversation with Lisa. She was puzzled, but she didn't want to ask anyone about what was confusing her.

Like Joanie, you and other young people hear your parents, teachers, and friends use words that are sometimes not familiar. You *think* you know what the words mean, but many times what you think is not correct. That's why this book was written. It will help you so you won't have the kinds of problems Joanie did. You will *know* the correct words and terms about your body and about sex and reproduction. For example, if you're not quite certain just what the word "reproduction" means, you can look it up under the "R's," just as you would in a regular dictionary. The illustrations, puzzles, word searches, and quizzes, have been added to the book to help you learn.

After you have read the definitions in this book, you may still have some questions. If so, go to a parent or your school health teacher or counselor, or go to the library or to a religious leader. Pick a responsible adult you know and trust. Then share your concerns. This is better than letting your questions go unanswered.

You can always come back to this book for specific definitions. It's meant to answer many of the questions you have about human sexuality and human reproduction. It's for you to use as you grow and change and experience the happiness of becoming a responsible young adult.

A

abdomen (AB-doe-men). The part of the body which houses, among other organs, the stomach, the intestines and, in a woman, the uterus or womb.

abortion (a-BORE-shun). The removal of an unborn embryo from a mother's uterus. This procedure is usually done in a doctor's office or a hospital and does not produce a baby.

abstinence (AB-stih-nens). Not indulging in an appetite or craving. The word can mean not having sexual relations.

acne (ACK-nee). Pimples; eruptions on the skin common during adolescence and sometimes caused by infections in the pores.

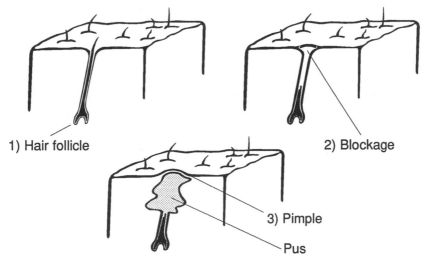

1) Hair follicle   2) Blockage

3) Pimple

Pus

Enlarged sections of skin.

Adam's Apple. The projection or bump on a boy's throat that gets bigger as he becomes a man. Girls have them, too, but they are seldom large. It's a part of the throat that contains the vocal chords.

Adam's apple ————————

adolescence (add-oh-LESS-ens). The time of life when a girl changes from a girl into a young woman and a boy changes from a boy into a young man. These changes usually begin to take place between ages 8 and 13 and can continue until a person is a legal adult.

adultery (ah-DULL-tree). Sexual intercourse between a married man and a partner other than his wife, or a married woman and a partner other than her husband.

affection. Caring for something or someone.

afterbirth. Shortly after a baby is born, the placenta, a temporary organ, is expelled from the mother. This is called the afterbirth. See placenta.

AIDS (Acquired Immune Deficiency Syndrome). A deadly viral disease that is transmitted in three ways: 1) by having sex with an infected person, 2) by sharing a drug needle with an infected person, or 3) by an infected mother passing the disease to her unborn baby. See immune system.

amniocentesis (AM-nee-oh-sen-TEE-sis). The process whereby a doctor inserts a hollow needle through the abdomen and into the uterus of a pregnant female and withdraws amniotic fluid. This can be done to determine the sex of the unborn child, to check chemicals that determine mature fetal lung development, or to check for abnormal chromosomes.

amniotic fluid (am-nee-AH-tik fluid). The fluid in which an unborn child lives inside the mother's uterus.

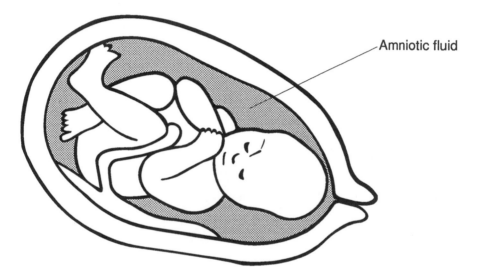

Amniotic fluid

amniotic sac (am-nee-AH-tik sac). A thin membrane that forms a closed sac around the fetus. It contains the amniotic fluid.

anal (A-nul) **intercourse**. The insertion of a man's penis into the anus of another person for sexual stimulation. See intercourse.

antibody (AN-tih-body). A protein produced in the blood in response to toxins or foreign organisms. In many cases, antibodies can neutralize toxins and help eliminate infections. In the case of AIDS, antibodies cannot combat the disease.

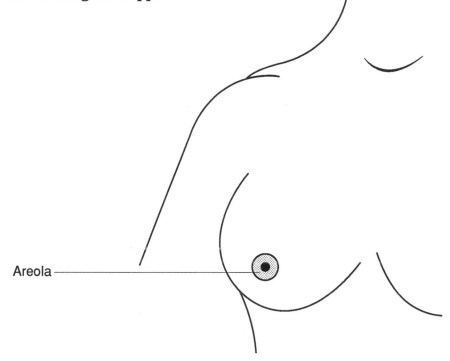

anus (A-nus). The opening in the body through which bowel movements pass.

areola (Ah-REE-oh-la). On the breast, the area of darkened skin surrounding the nipple.

Areola

arousal (uh-ROU-zal). Feelings of strong physical attraction towards another person.

artificial insemination (ar-tih-FISH-ul in-sem-ih-NAY-shun). Semen is placed into the vagina using a syringe rather than through intercourse.

B

baby. A newborn child.

baby blues. A period of depression some women experience for several weeks after the birth of a child.

basal body temperature. The temperature of the body when waking from sleep. A woman can keep track of this daily to help her determine when she has ovulated.

belly (see abdomen). Some children say a baby grows in the mother's belly, but this is not correct. The baby actually grows in the mother's uterus.

bellybutton (also called the navel). This is where the mother's umbilical cord is attached to a baby's body before the baby is born. Through the cord, the baby receives nourishment from the mother. After birth, the cord is no longer needed, so it is cut away. The spot where it is tied and cut away from the baby is the bellybutton or navel.

birth. The process that brings a baby into the world. After nine months in the uterus, the baby comes out of the mother's body through the birth canal.

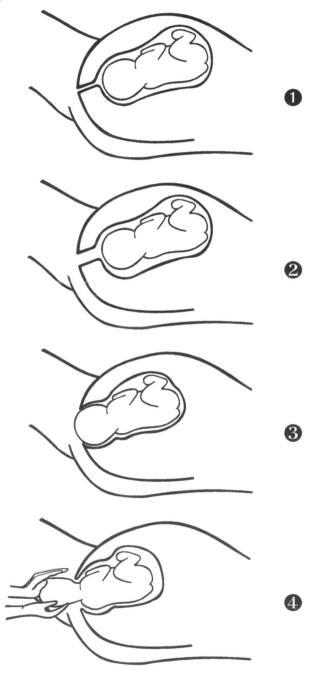

birth canal. The passage from the mother's uterus to the outside world—also called the vagina.

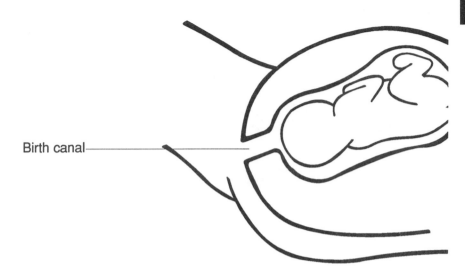

Birth canal

birth control. Any method used to prevent a baby from being conceived. One example is birth control pills.

birth control pills. Pills taken by a woman to prevent a baby from being conceived.

birth disorders. Problems infants may experience at the time of birth.

bisexual (by-SEK-shu-ul). Someone who is physically attracted to both sexes, male and female.

bladder. The sac in the body where urine is stored.

body fluids. Any fluids which exist normally in the body, such as blood, semen, and vaginal secretions.

bosom (BUHZ-em). Another name for a woman's breasts. In a man, bosom refers to the chest.

Bradley method. A method of natural childbirth developed by Dr. Robert Bradley. The technique emphasizes abdominal breathing techniques designed to help a mother relax during childbirth.

Braxton-Hicks Contractions. See false labor.

breast feeding. The feeding of a baby from a mother's breasts rather than from a bottle.

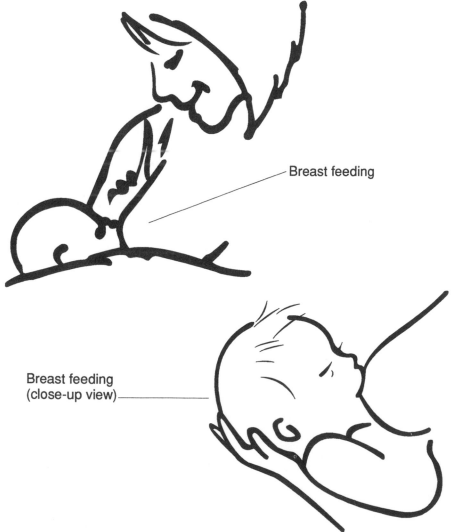

Breast feeding

Breast feeding
(close-up view)

Breast Self-Examination (BSE). A technique developed to help a woman check for lumps or changes in the breasts.

breasts (also called mammary glands). These begin to appear on a young girl sometime between ages 8 and 13. A mother's milk develops in them after a child is born. They are like two "baby bottles" designed by nature for the purpose of feeding a baby a "formula" created just for that special child.

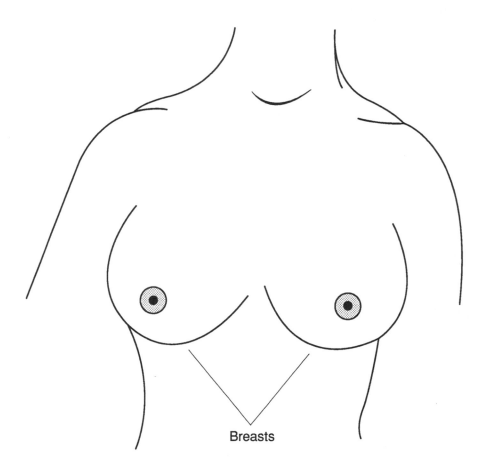

Breasts

breech birth. When a baby comes through the birth canal buttocks first.

buttocks. The rump; the part of the body on which a person sits.

C

C-section. See cesarean section.

calendar method. A method of birth control where a woman keeps track of the dates of her menstrual cycles. This helps her determine when she has ovulated and when she might be most likely to conceive, if intercourse occurs.

celibate (SELL-ih-but). Someone who abstains from sexual intercourse.

cell. A tiny, microscopic piece of matter capable of interacting with other cells to perform the functions of life.

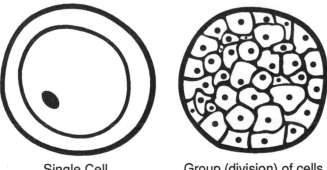

Single Cell   Group (division) of cells

cell division. The process by which cells multiply. Also the process by which a new baby is formed in the body of the mother.

cervical mucus (SER-vih-kal MYOO-kus). A sticky substance surrounding the opening of the cervix or neck of the womb.

cervical os (SER-vih-kal ohs) The opening of the cervix. See cervix.

C **cervix** (SER-vix). The narrow opening or neck of the uterus. It expands to allow a baby to be born. See sex organs.

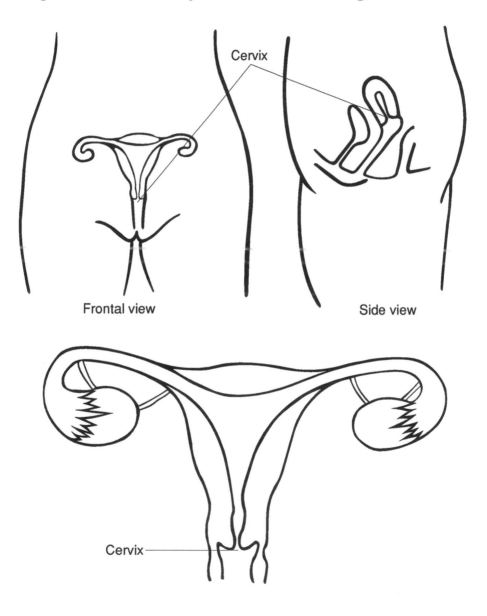

Cervix

Frontal view

Side view

Cervix

cesarean section (sez-AIR-ee-an section). Sometimes a baby is not able to be born naturally through the mother's vagina. An operation is necessary to remove the baby from the uterus through the mother's abdomen. This operation is called a cesarean section.

chancre (SHANK-er). A small sore or ulcer; can be a symptom of syphilis.

change of life. See menopause.

chaste, chastity (CHASED, CHASS-tih-tee). These words refer to someone who is modest, pure, innocent, or who does not have sexual relations before marriage.

chlamydia (kla-MIH-dee-ah). A germ that causes nongonococcal urethritis, a common sexually-transmitted disease—a leading cause of tubal damage and infertility.

chromosome (CHROME-o-zome). Part of a cell nucleus that contains the genes that make up an individual.

circumcision (sir-kum-SIH-shun). The removal of the foreskin from a baby boy's penis. A doctor performs this operation a few days after a boy is born. Not all parents decide to have this operation performed, so not all boys are circumcised. Circumcision is a religious custom in the Jewish faith.

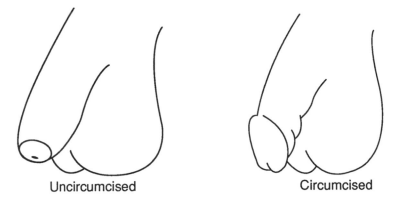

Uncircumcised   Circumcised

climax. See orgasm.

clitoris (KLIT-eh-res). A sensitive part of a woman's sexual organs similar to a tiny penis. See sex organs.

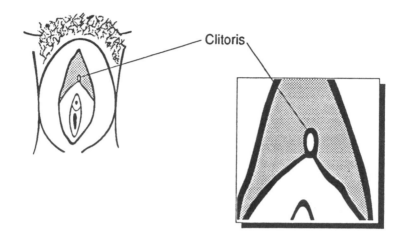

Clitoris

coitus (KOH-ih-tus or koh-EE-tus). Another name for sexual intercourse.

coitus interruptus (ko-EE-tus in-ter-UP-tus). The male withdraws his penis from the vagina just before ejaculation. This is also called withdrawal.

colostrum (koh-LOSS-trum). A substance produced by a mother's breasts shortly after a baby is born. It is healthy for the newborn baby to drink the colostrum before the mother's milk "comes in." This usually happens a few days after birth.

conceive (con-SEEV). To become pregnant.

conception (con-SEP-shun). The coming together of an egg cell from the mother and a sperm cell from the father. This is the beginning of the development of a new baby.

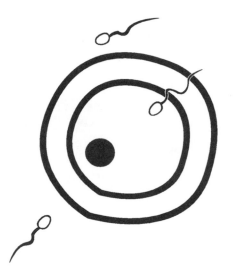

Sperm cell enters egg cell at moment of conception

condom (CON-dum). A soft rubber device that fits over a man's penis. It is worn during intercourse to prevent a baby from being conceived or to help prevent sexually-transmitted diseases.

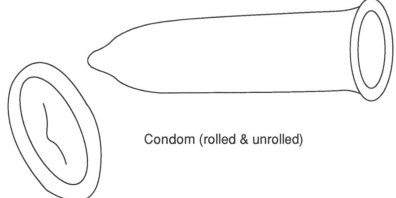

Condom (rolled & unrolled)

congenital (con-GEN-ih-tal). A condition existing at birth or acquired during development in the uterus—not an inherited trait or condition.

contraception (con-tra-SEP-shun). Preventing a baby from being conceived.

contraceptive (con-tra-SEP-tiv). Any of a number of methods used to prevent contraception, such as the IUD (intrauterine device), condoms, the diaphragm, the "pill," vasectomy, and tubal ligation.

contractions (con-TRACK-shuns). The workings of the muscles of the mother's uterus that get stronger and stronger before a baby is born. Contractions push a baby into the world. This effort on the mother's part is called labor.

copulation (cop-you-LAY-shun). Another name for sexual intercourse.

crabs or crab lice. Insects that get into the pubic hair and cause itching. Crabs can be passed from one person to another through genital contact.

D

DNA (deoxyribonucleic acid). A chemical in the body that is a basic component of genes. DNA determines what characteristics a baby will inherit from its parents and is sometimes called the "blueprint of life."

dating. A time when a girl and a boy, or a man and a woman, share each other's company.

DES (diethylstilbestrol). A potent estrogen-like medication taken within 72 hours after intercourse to prevent pregnancy.

diaphragm (DYE-a-fram). A rubber device a woman can place over the cervix to prevent pregnancy.

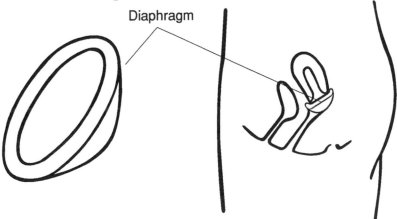

Diaphragm

differentiation (diff-er-en-she-A-shun). The complicated process used by the cells to develop the different body parts of a baby in the uterus.

dilation (die-LAY-shun). Refers to the opening of the cervix to allow a baby to be born.

dominant trait (DOM-in-ant trait). An inherited trait that overrides another trait such as brown eyes being inherited instead of blue eyes.

douche (DOOSH). A current of water, or a commercial solution used to cleanse a body cavity—usually the vagina.

D

E

EDC (estimated date of confinement). The approximate time that the delivery of a baby will occur.

ectopic pregnancy (eck-TOP-ik pregnancy). The abnormal implantation of a fertile ovum outside the mother's uterus, such as in the fallopian tube. See tubal pregnancy.

egg cell (also called ovum). The part of a baby that is produced in the mother's ovaries. Two cells are needed to produce a baby: an egg cell from the mother's ovaries, and a sperm cell from the father's testicles. Each cell contains a set of chromosomes and, when these two cells unite, the very first cell of a new baby is produced.

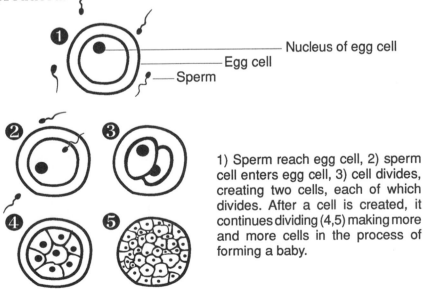

Nucleus of egg cell
Egg cell
Sperm

1) Sperm reach egg cell, 2) sperm cell enters egg cell, 3) cell divides, creating two cells, each of which divides. After a cell is created, it continues dividing (4,5) making more and more cells in the process of forming a baby.

ejaculation (ee-JACK-u-lay-shun). The spurting of semen or sperm from a man's penis.

embryo (EM-bree-oh). An unborn baby from conception to three months. After three months, the unborn child is referred to as a fetus.

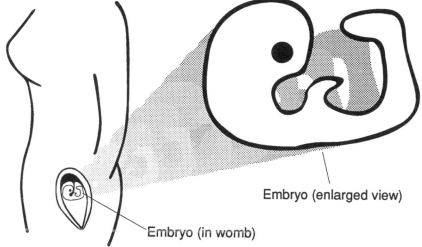

Embryo (enlarged view)

Embryo (in womb)

emotions (ee-MOE-shuns). Changing thoughts, moods, and feelings that are particularly pronounced during adolescence and also during menopause.

endometrium (en-doe-ME-tree-um). The velvety lining of the uterus in which a fertilized egg develops.

environment (en-VYE-run-ment). The conditions in which a person grows and develops and by which a person is surrounded.

epididymis (ep-ih-DID-ih-mus). Tiny tubes located behind each testicle in which sperm cells mature.

epidural block (ep-ih-DUR-al block). A form of local anesthesia administered to the lower portion of the mother's body during childbirth to reduce pain.

episiotomy (ee-pee-zee-AH-tah-mee). A surgical incision made at the time of birth to allow the baby to pass from the vagina more easily.

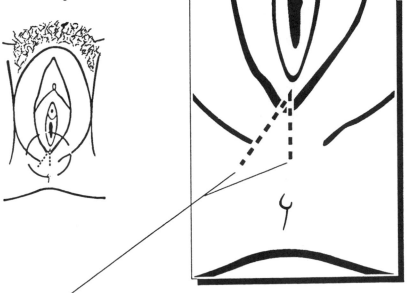

Episiotomy incision is made either towards the anus or sideways

erection (ee-RECK-shun). The enlargement and hardening of a man's penis which makes sexual intercourse possible.

erotic (ee-RAH-tic). Meant to or tending to arouse sexual desire or strongly affected by sexual desire.

estrogen (ESS-tro-gen). The female sex hormone produced in a woman's ovaries. It affects the menstrual cycle and the development of a woman's sexual characteristics.

expulsion (ex-PUL-shun). To force out. A fetus is sometimes expelled from the uterus causing a miscarriage.

E

F

fallopian tubes (fah-LOW-pee-an tubes). Part of a woman's sexual organs through which the egg cells pass from the ovaries to the uterus. The egg cell and sperm cell meet in the fallopian tube when conception occurs. The fertilized egg cell then moves to the uterus. See sex organs.

Fallopian tubes

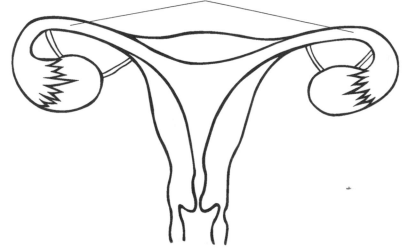

false labor. Pains a mother may experience when a baby is about to be born that are not actual labor pains—also called Braxton-Hicks contractions.

family planning. The decisions parents make about how many children to have and when they would like to have them.

fantasy. A dream; not real.

father. The male partner who, along with the mother, brings children into the world.

female (FEE-male). A girl or woman.

fertile (FUR-til). Physically able to produce children.

fertility (fur-TIL-ih-tee). Being fertile.

fertility awareness method. A method of birth control based on a woman's being able to recognize her fertile time of the month. She then can use a barrier method, such as a diaphragm, during those times when fertilization is most likely to occur.

fertilization (fur-till-eye-ZA-shun). The meeting of a sperm cell and an egg cell—the beginning of a new life.

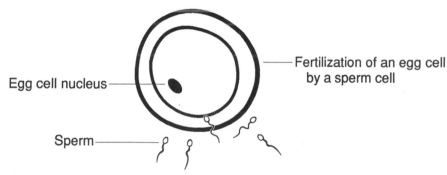

Egg cell nucleus

Fertilization of an egg cell by a sperm cell

Sperm

fetal alcohol syndrome (FEE-tahl). A serious disorder in babies born to mothers who drink alcohol heavily while they are pregnant. It causes mental retardation and deformities.

fetoscopy (fee-TAH-scop-ee). Direct examination of the fetus using a fetoscope or thin tube containing a scope.

fetus (FEE-tus). An unborn baby from the third month after conception until birth.

fimbria (FIM-bree-ah). The fringes at the end of each fallopian tube that help draw an egg cell into the tube on its way to the uterus.

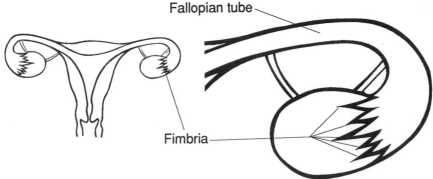

Fallopian tube

Fimbria

foam. A type of contraceptive used in a woman's vagina.

follicles (FALL-ick-els). Small sacs in the ovaries that contain egg cells. Also refers to male sperm follicles.

follicle stimulating hormone (FSH). A hormone produced by the pituitary gland in both males and females. FSH causes either the female egg follicle or the male sperm follicle to mature.

fontanel (fon-ton-ELL). The membrane-covered soft spot in a newborn baby's head which closes a few weeks after birth.

Fontanel (soft spot)

View of top of skull

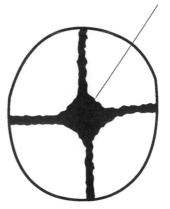

foreplay (FOR-play). The kissing and touching that take place before intercourse.

foreskin (FOR-skin). The skin covering the tip of the penis. This skin is removed, if a boy is circumcised.

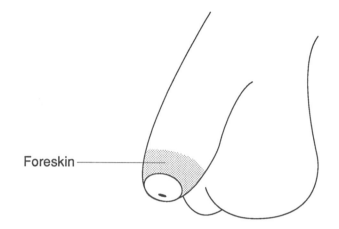

Foreskin

fornication (for-nih-KAY-shun). Sexual relations between unmarried people.

fraternal twins (frah-TER-nal twins). Twins produced by two egg cells meeting with two sperm cells. See also identical twins.

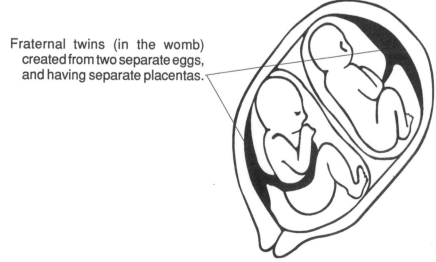

Fraternal twins (in the womb) created from two separate eggs, and having separate placentas.

G

gay. See homosexual.

gender (GEN-der). Sex; either male or female.

gender identity (GEN-der eye-DEN-tih-tee). Filling the role of either a male or a female.

genes (JEENZ). The tiny units of heredity carried by the chromosomes.

genetics (jen-ETT-icks). The science of heredity—how traits are passed by the genes from one generation to another.

genital herpes (JEN-ih-tal HER-pees). A type of viral venereal disease that produces sores on the sexual organs.

genital warts (JEN-ih-tal warts). A sexually-transmitted disease caused by a virus, resulting in small warts on and around the sex organs.

genitals (JEN-ih-tals). Usually refers to the external sexual organs of a male or a female. See sex organs.

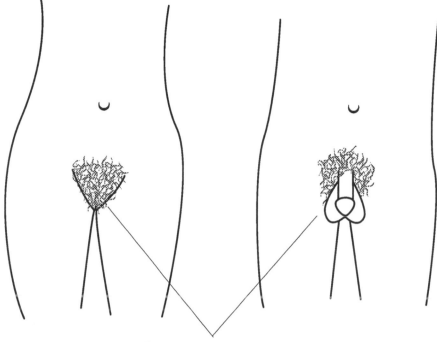

Genitals (female & male)

genetic counseling. The application of what is known about human genetics to problems that may arise during a pregnancy.

German measles (Rubella). A disease a pregnant woman may contract that can cause deafness in an unborn child.

gestation (jes-TAY-shun). The nine-month period during which a baby develops inside its mother's uterus.

glans. The extreme end of the penis. Glans can also refer to the tip of the female clitoris. See sex organs.

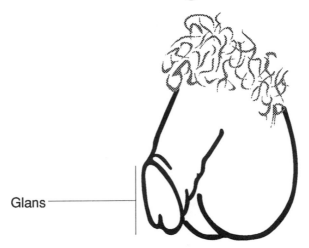

Glans

gonococcus (gone-oh-KAH-kus). A germ that causes gonorrhea.

gonorrhea (gone-oh-REE-ah). A common, yet serious, sexually-transmitted disease.

growth spurt. Refers to a period in a girl or boy's life when they suddenly grow taller and begin to develop rapidly.

gynecological exam (guy-nah-co-LODGE-ih-kal exam). Examination by a doctor of a woman's external genitals as well as the vagina and cervix.

gynecologist (guy-nah-CALL-oh-jist). A doctor who specializes in all areas of female medicine.

gynecology (guy-nah-CALL-oh-gee). The branch of medicine that deals with the diseases and hygiene of women.

H

heat. Fertile time in female cycle; refers mainly to animals.

hemoglobin (HE-mah-glow-bin). An iron-containing pigment occurring in the blood stream.

hemorrhoids (HEM-or-oids). A mass of swollen, dilated veins near or inside the anal opening caused by straining to have a bowel movement. Hemorrhoids also may occur due to the pushing a woman exerts when giving birth to a child.

heredity (her-ED-ih-tee). The characteristics parents pass from one generation to the other through the genes.

herpes (see also genital herpes). Viral diseases of the skin. Some are sexually-transmitted. Some are not.

heterosexual (het-er-oh-SEX-ual). A person who is attracted to someone of the opposite sex.

homophobia (hoe-moe-FOE-bee-ah). Fear of homosexuals and homosexuality.

homosexual (hoe-moe-SEX-you-al). A person who is sexually attracted to someone of the same sex.

hormones (HOR-moans). Chemicals secreted by the glands, some of which produce sexual differences between men and women.

hot flash. Also called hot flush. A sudden, brief sensation of heat felt by women going through menopause. A hot flash is caused by the dilation of skin capillaries and can be felt several times a day for a year or more.

hygiene (HIGH-jeen). Keeping the body parts clean and healthy.

hymen (HIGH-men). A layer of tissue (or membrane) covering or partially covering the opening of the vagina. If present, the hymen may be broken by intercourse, by surgical incision, or by the use of tampons. See sex organs.

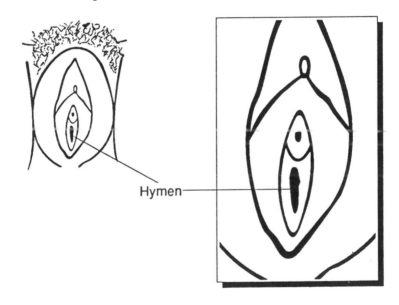

Hymen

hysterectomy (hist-er-ECK-tah-mee). an operation performed on a woman to remove her uterus. Without a uterus she cannot bear children.

I

IUD (intrauterine device). A metal or plastic birth control device that a doctor can place in a woman's uterus through the vagina.

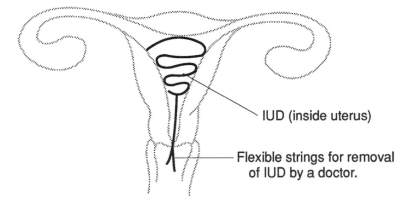

IUD (inside uterus)

Flexible strings for removal of IUD by a doctor.

identical twins (eye-DENT-ick-al twins). Two babies that are started by the same fertilized egg which then divides into two parts. See also fraternal twins.

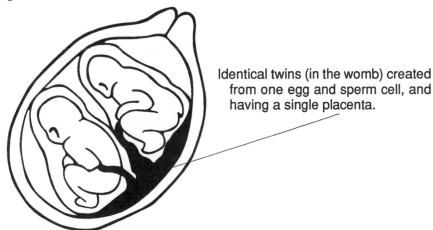

Identical twins (in the womb) created from one egg and sperm cell, and having a single placenta.

illegitimate child (ill-la-JIT-ah-mut child). Traditionally refers to a child born to parents who are not married.

immoral (im-MORE-al). Going against commonly held moral principles; sometimes refers to being unchaste or having sexual relations before marriage.

implantation (im-plant-TA-shun). The process of attachment of the embryo to the mother's uterine wall where it begins to grow and develop.

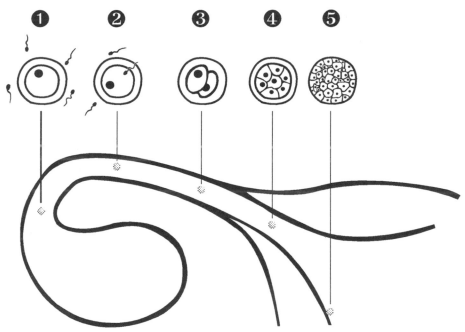

Fertilized egg (1) travels from ovary through fallopian tube (2,3,4) until it reaches the uterus, where it attaches to the mother's uterine wall (5).

immune system. The body's defense system against disease. In AIDS, the immune system cannot combat the infection.

impotent (IM-pet-ent). Lacking power or strength—unable to have sexual intercourse due to failure of the erection of the penis.

in vitro fertilization. Fertilization of an egg cell by a sperm cell outside a woman's body under laboratory conditions. The fertilized egg cell is then inserted into the uterus.

incest (IN-sest). Sexual intercourse between people who are so closely related they are forbidden by law to marry each other, such as between a father and daughter or between a brother and sister.

infant mortality. Baby deaths caused by many different factors.

infatuation (in-FAT-u-ay-shun). A foolish or extravagant love or affection for another person.

I

infertility (in-fer-TILL-i-tee). The inability to produce children. Either a man or a woman may be infertile.

inherited traits. Traits parents pass on to their children, such as height, weight, and hair color.

instinct (IN-stinkt). A natural, inborn impulse.

intercourse (IN-ter-korse). Can mean any interaction or communication. In sexual terms, it usually refers to the mating of a man and a woman. This involves the insertion of a man's penis into a woman's vagina and is called vaginal intercourse. During vaginal intercourse a baby may be, but is not always, conceived.

intimate (IN-tih-mut). Very personal or private. Intimate relations sometimes refers to sexual relations between a man and a woman.

intrauterine device (in-tra-YOU-ter-in). See IUD.

J

jealous (JEL-uhs). Being fearful of losing another person's love or affection.

K

kinky. Appealing to strange or unusual tastes, especially in regard to sexual matters.

kiss. A caress of the lips—an expression of affection.

L

labia (LAY-bee-eh). Part of the external female genitals. Labia is Latin, meaning lips. See sex organs.

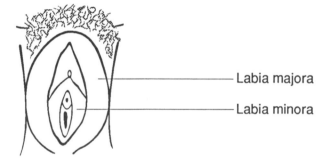

labia majora (LAY-bee-eh meh-JOR-eh). The outer folds of the vulva.

labia minora (LAY-bee-eh meh-NOR-eh). The inner folds of the vulva.

labor. The effort a mother puts forth during childbirth to bring a baby into the world. Contractions are part of the labor process.

lactogenesis (lack-toe-GEN-eh-sis). When milk production begins in a mother's breasts shortly after birth.

LaLeche League (la-LAY-chee). An organization formed to help nursing mothers. LaLeche is Spanish for "the milk."

Lamaze (lah-MAHZ). A method of childbirth involving the physical and psychological preparation of the mother. It helps suppress pain and often allows the mother to deliver the baby without the use of drugs.

laparoscopy (lap-ah-RAH-scop-ee). A procedure using a fiber-optic telescope which allows a physician to view the pelvic organs. Used mostly for diagnosing problems or for sterilization.

L

Leboyer method (Lah-BOY-er method). A natural childbirth method developed by Frederick Leboyer. The newborn baby is delivered in a quiet, dimly lit room and placed immediately on its mother's abdomen. Then the baby is placed in warm water and rocked gently.

lesbian (LEZ-bee-un). A female homosexual.

loop. See IUD.

love. The great and powerful force and emotion that draws people together. Physical love between a man and a woman often results in the birth of a new human being.

M

macho (MAH-choh). Spanish for male or masculine. Machismo (ma-CHEESE-mo) is a term meaning that a father is man enough to provide for all the children he has.

maidenhead. Refers to the hymen. Also refers to being a maiden or virgin. See hymen.

male. A boy or man.

mammary glands. Another name for female breasts.

M

Mammary gland
(inside breast)

marriage. The state of being married; the legal and lawful union of a husband and wife usually for the purpose of founding and maintaining a family.

masturbate (MASS-tur-bate). To self-stimulate the sexual organs.

mate. A spouse or close companion. **Mating** refers to sexual intercourse.

maternal (ma-TER-nal). Having to do with a mother.

menarche (MEN-ar-kee). A girl's first menstrual period.

menopause (MEN-oh-pauz). A time in a woman's life when the ovaries stop producing egg cells and hormones and when menstruation ceases—sometimes called the "change of life."

M

menstrual cramps (MEN-stroo-al cramps). The painful feelings some females experience in their lower abdomen during their menstrual period.

menstrual cycle. The monthly fertility cycle most women experience beginning with the first day of menstruation and continuing for about a month until the next cycle begins.

menstrual period (MEN-stroo-al period). Normally, the three-to-six day period when menstruation takes place. A girl can begin having menstrual periods as early as age eight.

menstruation (MEN-stroo-AY-shun). The monthly discharge of blood from a girl's or woman's uterus. Menstruation occurs approximately every 28 days. If a baby is conceived, menstruation stops during the nine-month pregnancy period and then resumes again after the baby is born.

Uterus before menstruation

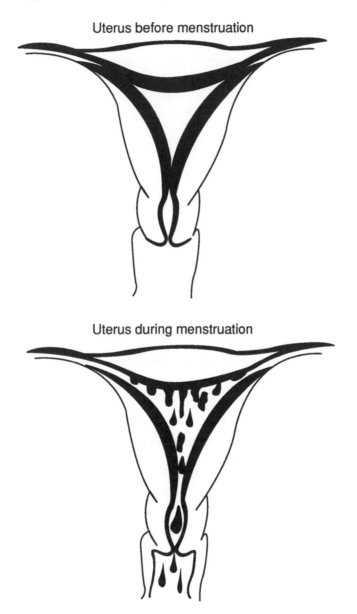

Uterus during menstruation

M

midwife. A person who helps women during childbirth.

milk. The nourishing liquid produced by a mother's breasts following the birth of a baby.

miscarriage (MIS-care-ij). The loss of an embryo from the uterus—especially during the first three months of pregnancy.

molester (moh-LESS-ter). Usually refers to a child molester—someone who abuses or harms a child.

monogamy (mah-NOG-ah-me). Marrying only once during a lifetime or having only one marriage partner at a time.

mons pubis (mons PU-bis). In females, the rounded, soft area above the pubic bone.

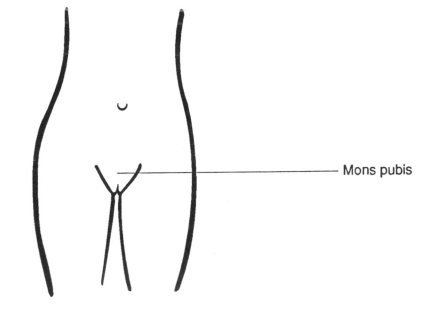

Mons pubis

morality (more-AL-ih-tee). Living by high moral principles—sometimes refers to being chaste or not having sexual intercourse before marriage.

morning-after pill. A strong estrogen pill taken 24 to 72 hours after intercourse to prevent pregnancy. It sometimes causes vomiting, headaches, and diarrhea.

morning sickness. Nausea and vomiting experienced by many women during the early months of pregnancy.

mother. The female partner who, along with a father, brings children into the world.

mucus (MYOO-kus). A sticky substance produced by various body parts, including a woman's cervix.

M

N

natural birth control or natural family planning. A method of birth control based on a woman's learning to recognize her fertile time of the month. Intercourse is then avoided during these days.

natural childbirth. The birth of a baby where no anesthesia is used.

nausea (NAH-zee-ah or NAH-zha). Feeling sick to the stomach. See morning sickness.

navel. The small scar on the abdomen where the umbilical cord was detached at the time of birth. See also bellybutton.

N

necking. A term used to describe a couple sitting close together, kissing, and touching one another for the purposes of sexual pleasure.

newborn. A newly born baby.

nipple. The tip of a woman's breast. It performs the same function as the nipple on a baby bottle. The baby sucks on it and nurses or draws milk from its mother.

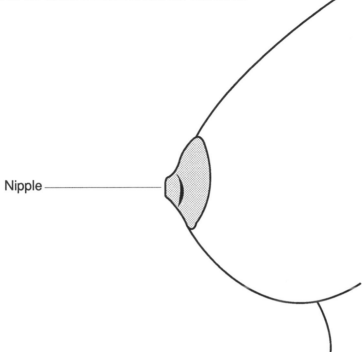

Nipple

nocturnal emission (knock-TURN-all ee-MISH-un). The release of sperm from the penis during the nighttime and/or during a dream. Nocturnal emissions usually begin when a boy is 13 or 14 years old. Also called "wet dream."

nongonococcal urethritis (nahn-gahn-uh-KAH-kul yer-eh-THRY-tus)—**NGU**. A sexually-transmitted disease (not gonorrhea).

Nonoxynol-9 (non-OX-in-ol-9). A spermacide and disease-killing chemical used in contraceptive products. May be in cream, foam, or jelly form.

nurse. To draw nourishment from a mother's breast. See breastfeeding.

O

obstetrician (ob-sta-TRIH-shun). A doctor who delivers babies and takes care of medical problems associated with pregnancy.

offspring. Children.

oral sex or oral intercourse (OR-ul). The placement of the mouth on the genitals of another person for sexual stimulation. See intercourse.

orgasm (OR-gaz-um). The climax of sexual pleasure during intercourse.

os (ohs). The opening of the uterus.

out of wedlock. Traditionally refers to a child born to a woman who is not married.

ova (OH-vah). Egg cells in the female. Plural of ovum.

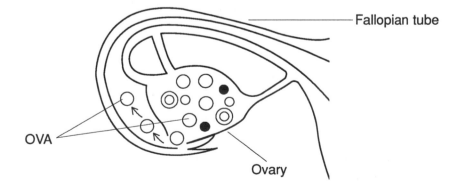

Fallopian tube

OVA

Ovary

ovaducts (OH-vah-ducts). See fallopian tubes.

ovarian cyst (oh-VAR-ee-an sist). An abnormal growth on the ovary.

ovaries. Plural for ovary.

ovary (OH-vah-ree). The organ in the female where egg cells and sex hormones are produced and stored. See sex organs.

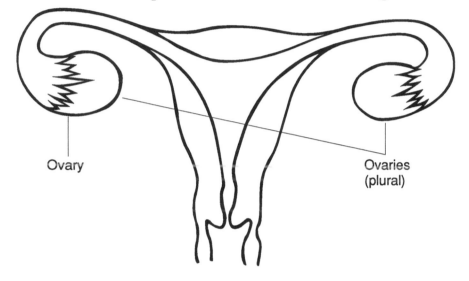

Ovary

Ovaries
(plural)

ovulation (ahv-u-LAY-shun). The release of an egg cell from the ovary which occurs in a female about once a month. Ovulation may begin as early as age 8. The egg cell travels through the fallopian tube to the uterus. There it is either fertilized by a sperm cell or expelled through menstruation.

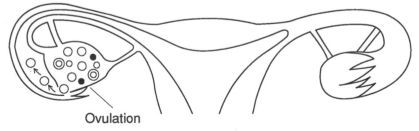

Ovulation

ovum (OH-vum). A female egg cell. See egg cell.

P

PAP test or PAP smear. A routine test performed in a doctor's office to test for cancer in the female reproductive organs.

paracervical block (para-SERVE-ick-al block). A local anesthetic injected near the cervix (or neck of the uterus) to reduce pain during labor.

parenting. The skills used by a mother and father in bearing and rearing children.

parturition (par-chur-IH-shun). The action or process of giving birth to offspring.

passion (PASH-un). An extremely compelling emotion; can refer to love or anger.

paternal (pa-TER-nal). Having to do with a father.

pelvic inflamatory disease (PEL-vic in-FLAM-ah-tory disease) **or PID**. A bacteria-caused infection that travels from the vagina or cervix to the uterus and fallopian tubes. PID can cause infertility.

pelvis (PEL-vis). The basin-shaped structure in the body formed by the pelvic girdle and bones of the spine.

penis (PEE-nis). The principal male sexual organ. See sex organs.

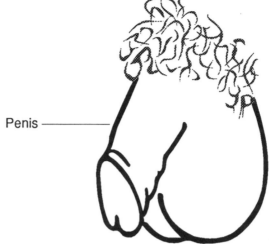

Penis —

penis shaft. The main length of the penis made up of erectile tissue covered by skin.

perinatal (pair-ih-NAY-tal). Pertaining to or occuring during the period before or shortly after birth.

period. See menstrual period.

P

perineum (per-eh-NEE-em). Usually refers to the area of the female anatomy located between the vagina and the anus. See sex organs.

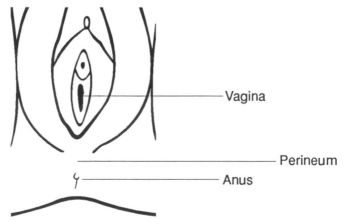

Vagina

Perineum

Anus

pervert (PUR-vert). A person who commits unnatural sexual acts.

petting. Touching someone else's body to arouse sexual pleasure.

physical traits. What we inherit from our parents such as eye color, hair color, height, and weight.

pill. See birth control pills.

pimples. Small, inflamed spots on the skin common in boys and girls of adolescent age—also called acne or zits.

pituitary gland (pih-TOO-ah-tair-ee gland). A tiny gland at the base of the brain that controls the other glands in the body. During adolescence it begins the process of changing a girl into a young woman and a boy into a young man.

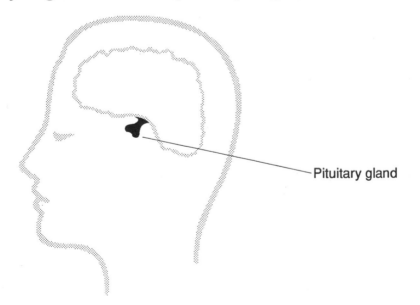

Pituitary gland

P

placenta (pluh-CENT-ah). A temporary, waffle-shaped organ that exchanges nutrients and wastes between the mother and the fetus. The placenta also produces hormones necessary to maintain pregnancy. See afterbirth.

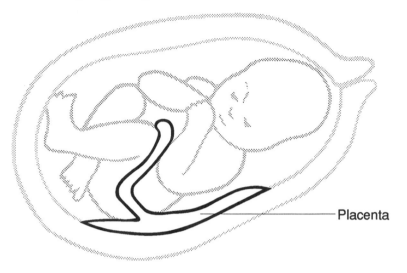

Placenta

polygamy (pah-LIG-ah-me). Marriage in which the male may have more than one wife or the female may have more than one husband.

P **pornography** (por-NAH-gra-fee). Books, magazines, videos, and other material that show erotic material for the purpose of sexual excitement.

postpartum (post-PAR-tum). The time following the birth of a child.

postpartum depression. See baby blues.

preemie. A premature baby.

pregnancy. The nine-month period following conception when a baby develops inside its mother's uterus.

pregnant. A word used to describe a woman who is carrying an unborn child inside her uterus.

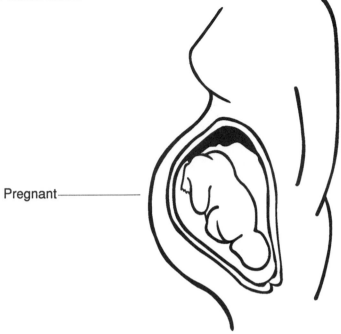

Pregnant

premarital intercourse (pree-MARE-it-al intercourse). Having sexual relations before marriage.

premature baby. A baby born before the full nine months of the mother's pregnancy, usually weighing under five pounds.

prenatal (pre-NAY-tal). The time or period before birth.

prenatal care (pre-NAY-tal care). The health care given to a mother during her pregnancy.

prepuce (PRE-pyoos). Can refer either to the foreskin of the penis or a similar fold of skin covering the clitoris.

preventive behavior. Behavior that gives at least some protection against spreading sexually-transmitted diseases.

P

progesterone (pro-JESS-ter-ohn). The female sex hormone which prepares a woman's uterus to receive and sustain a fertilized egg—sometimes called the "pregnancy hormone." It also causes a mother's breasts to produce milk for a newborn baby.

prostate gland. A gland surrounding the male urethra. From it comes a milky fluid, part of the semen. The muscles around the urethra are the main source of ejaculation.

prostatitis (pros-tah-TITE-us). Inflamation of the prostate.

puberty (PYOO-ber-tee). The years between approximately 10 and 13 when girls begin to change into young women and boys begin to change into young men. These changes happen at different times for every boy and girl. See also adolescence.

pubic hair (PYOO-bic). Hair surrounding the sexual organs of a girl or a boy. This hair develops during adolescence. See sex organs.

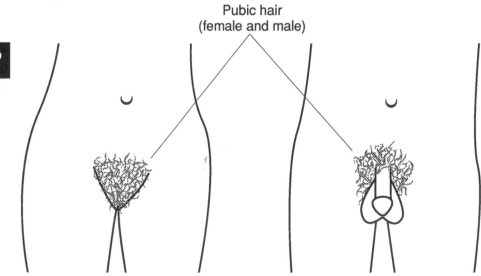

Pubic hair
(female and male)

pudendum (pyoo-DEN-dum). The external sexual organs of a human being, especially of a woman.

Q

quickening. The time during a mother's pregnancy when she first begins to feel the movement of the baby in the uterus—usually occurs about the fourth or fifth month.

R

rape. The crime of sexual intercourse with a woman by a man without her consent and usually by force. Rape can also refer to sexual intercourse by force or threat other than by a man with a woman, such as between a man and a boy.

Rh incompatibility (R-H in-come-pat-ih-BIL-it-ee). A mother may have Rh-negative blood and her baby Rh-positive. The mother's blood produces antibodies that may endanger future pregnancies. However, a solution of gamma globulin may be given to the mother to help correct the problem.

recessive (re-CESS-ive) **trait**. One that is not dominant. See dominant trait.

reproduction (ree-pro-DUK-shun) The process of reproducing. In humans, reproduction refers to the process of mating and giving birth to children.

reproductive (ree-pro-DUK-tive) **organs**. The organs in the body of a man or a woman that have to do with producing children.

response (ree-SPONS). Relating to another person or reacting to the invitation to relate to someone.

rhythm method (RIH-them method). See calendar method.

risky behavior. Behavior that may lead to a sexually-transmitted disease such as AIDS.

romance (ro-MANS). Love or passion.

romantic love. An intimate or passionate love.

rubber. See condom.

rubella. See German measles.

rut. Sexual excitement, especially when periodic. The term also refers to the annual, or yearly, state of sexual arousal in the male deer.

S

saddle block. A type of anesthesia given by injection into the lower spinal area to block pain during labor and delivery.

safe behavior. Behavior that prevents sexually-transmitted diseases.

safer sex. Sexual activity that helps to protect a person from AIDS or other sexually-transmitted diseases. In safer sex, no body fluids are shared.

sanitary napkin. A commercial pad of absorbent material worn by a female during her menstrual period to absorb the menstrual flow.

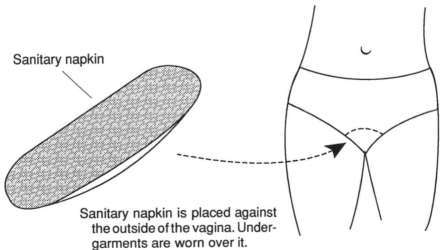

Sanitary napkin

Sanitary napkin is placed against the outside of the vagina. Undergarments are worn over it.

scrotum (SKRO-tum). The sac under the penis containing the testicles. See sex organs.

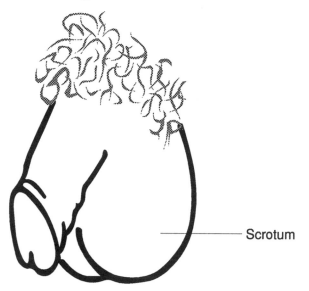

Scrotum

sebaceous glands (see-BAY-shus glands). Glands that secrete an oily material under the skin. These glands are particularly active during adolescence.

sebum (SEE-bem). Fatty lubricant matter secreted by the sebaceous glands of the skin. Sometimes associated with acne.

secondary sexual characteristics. The changes that occur in a young person's body during adolescence such as the development of hair under the arms, pubic hair, a deepening voice in boys, developing breasts in girls, etc.

seed. Sometimes refers to sperm cells.

self-control. In a sexual sense, acting responsibly—not giving in to impulsive actions. See safe behavior.

semen (SEE-mun). The fluid in a male which contains sperm. Semen is ejaculated from the penis.

seminal vesicles (SEM-in-al VESS-ick-als). Two sacs in a male's body where semen is stored. See sex organs.

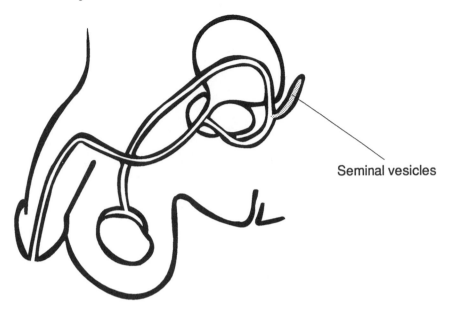

Seminal vesicles

seminiferous tubules (sem-in-IF-er-us TU-byuls). Structures located in the testes that produce sperm.

sex. Male or female or the attraction between the two.

sex organs. The major sexual organ for a boy is his penis—for a girl, her vagina. See illustrations on pages 72 and 73.

sex role. The way a society indicates how a man or a woman ought to behave. Also refers to what is expected of a mother or a father.

sexual characteristics. Those characteristics which distinguish a man from a woman. (See secondary sexual characteristics).

sexual intercourse. See intercourse.

FEMALE SEX ORGANS

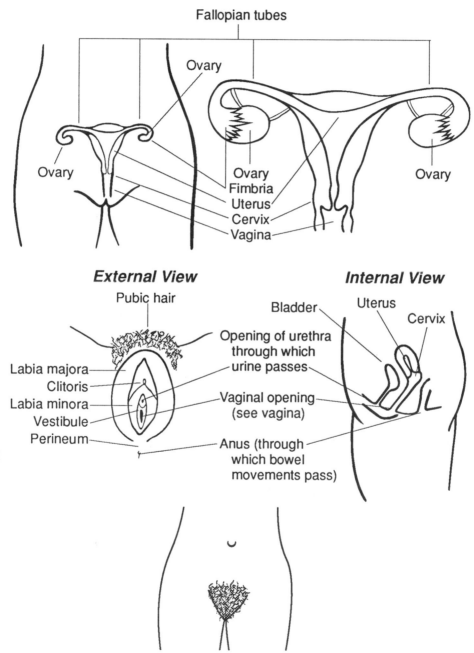

Internal View

Fallopian tubes

Ovary

Ovary

Ovary
Fimbria
Uterus
Cervix
Vagina

Ovary

External View

Pubic hair

Labia majora
Clitoris
Labia minora
Vestibule
Perineum

Opening of urethra
through which
urine passes

Vaginal opening
(see vagina)

Anus (through
which bowel
movements pass)

Internal View

Bladder

Uterus

Cervix

S

MALE SEX ORGANS

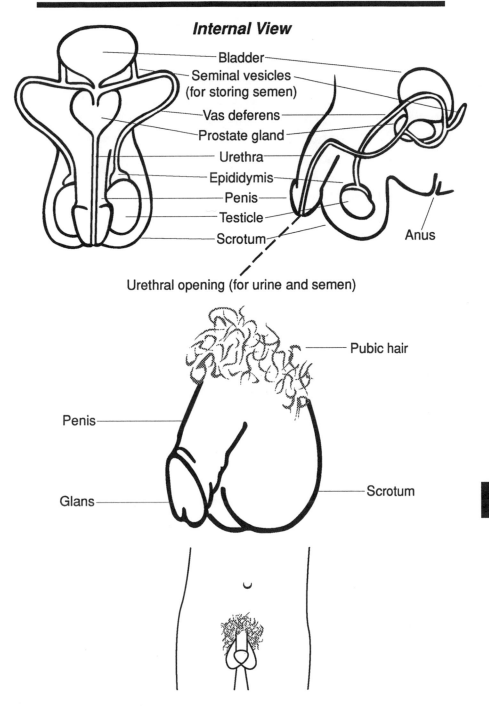

Internal View

Bladder

Seminal vesicles
(for storing semen)

Vas deferens

Prostate gland

Urethra

Epididymis

Penis

Testicle

Scrotum

Anus

Urethral opening (for urine and semen)

Pubic hair

Penis

Scrotum

Glans

S

sexual intimacy. The expression of physical feeling through sexual behavior.

sexuality. Our sexual nature—having to do with being a girl or a boy, a woman or a man. Can refer to sexual activity.

sexually transmitted diseases (STD). Diseases that may result from sexual intercourse or other intimate contact—also called venereal diseases. These diseases almost never occur between a husband and wife who have never had sexual partners other than each other.

sexy. Sexually attractive or interesting.

smegma (SMEG-mah). A thick, white substance that collects under the foreskin of a uncircumcised boy, if the foreskin is not pulled back and kept clean. This substance can cause odor and irritation. Smegma also collects under the foreskin of a girl's clitoris. These areas need to be cleaned daily with soap and water.

socially responsible person. Someone who cares about others. In sexual terms, someone who tries to prevent unwanted pregnancies and the spread of sexually-transmitted diseases.

sodomy (SAW-duh-mee). Anciently the homosexual activities of the men of the city of Sodom in the Old Testament. Sodomy can also refer to sex with an animal or to oral or anal copulation.

S

sperm (or sperm cell). The male reproductive cell. When a sperm cell from the father meets with an egg cell from the mother during intercourse, a baby may be conceived.

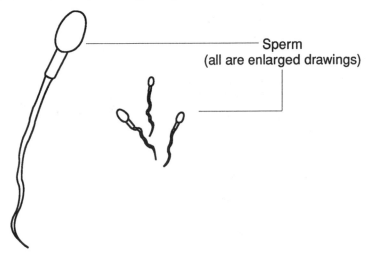

Sperm
(all are enlarged drawings)

spermacide (SPER-ma-side). A substance that kills sperm cells.

spermatozoa (sper-MA-tah-zoh-ah). The scientific name for sperm cells.

spirochete (SPY-ro-keets). Slender corkscrew-shaped bacteria that cause syphilis.

sponge. A soft plastic birth control device containing sperm-killing chemicals. A woman places the sponge in her vagina before intercourse to prevent pregnancy.

sterility (ster-ILL-eh-tee). Being sterile or unable to have children.

sterilization (ster-ill-eye-ZAY-shun). A surgical procedure that prevents a man from becoming a father or a woman from becoming a mother.

sweat glands. Glands, particularly under the arms, that become more active during adolescence. Greater body odor is normal as a young person matures, and greater effort is needed to keep the body clean.

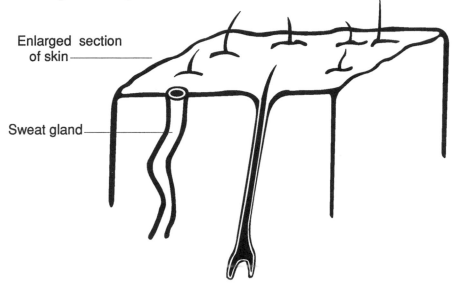

Enlarged section of skin

Sweat gland

syphilis (SIH-fill-iss). A serious but curable venereal disease.

T

tampon (TAM-pawn). A small roll of absorbent cotton a girl or woman inserts into her vagina to absorb menstrual flow.

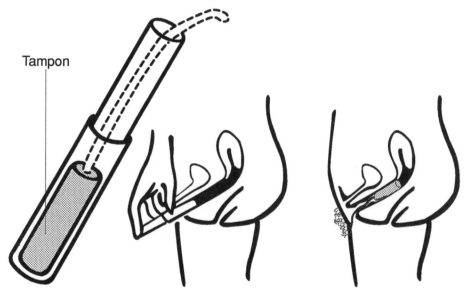

Tampon

teratogen (teh-RAT-eh-gen). A substance that causes birth defects or other diseases in humans.

test tube baby. A baby conceived by the bringing together of a sperm cell and an egg cell in a test tube. The fertilized egg cell can then be placed in the mother's uterus where it can grow and develop. See also artificial insemination.

testes (TES-teez). Plural for testicle.

testicle (TES-tick-al). An oval-shaped gland in a boy's scrotum that produces sperm cells. See sex organs.

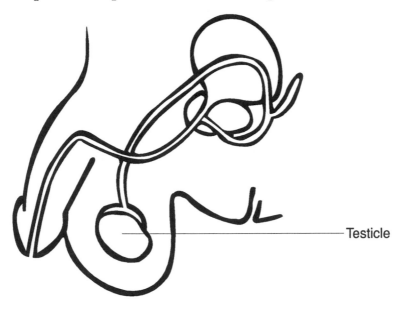

Testicle

testicular self-examination (tes-TIC-u-lar self-examination) **or TSE**. A technique for examining the testicles for lumps or other abnormalities.

testosterone (tes-TOSS-ter-ohn). A hormone produced in a boy's testicles which causes him, during adolescence, to develop his male sexual characteristics.

Toxic Shock Syndrome (TSS). A condition among women caused by staph bacteria in relation to the usage of tampons during the menstrual cycle. It is thought that not changing tampons frequently enough is a factor.

transmission (trans-MIH-shun). The process of transmitting or passing along. In the context of disease, transmission refers to passing something from one person to another.

trichomonas (trik-oh-MOE-nus). A common sexually-transmitted disease.

trimester (try-MESS-ter). A three-month period of time. The nine months of a woman's pregnancy are divided into the first, second, and third trimesters.

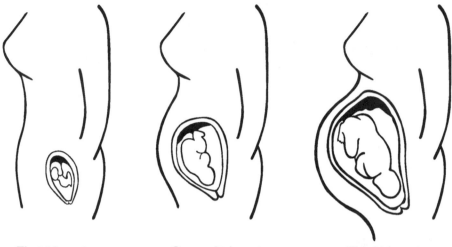

First trimester   Second trimester   Third trimester

tubal ligation (TOO-bell-lye-GAY-shun). A surgical procedure used to tie a woman's fallopian tubes to prevent pregnancy.

Tubal ligation

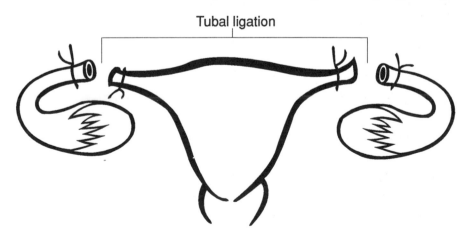

T

tubal pregnancy (TU-bel pregnancy). A serious condition that occurs when a fertilized egg begins to develop inside a mother's fallopian tube instead of inside the uterus.

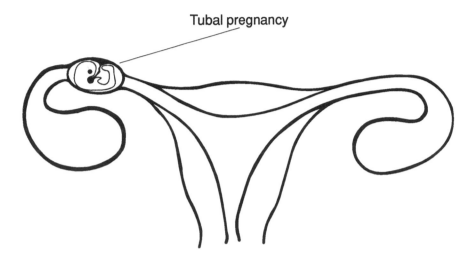

Tubal pregnancy

twin. Either of two offspring produced at birth. See identical and fraternal twins.

U

ultrasound. Vibrations of the same physical nature as sound, but the frequencies are above the range of human hearing. Ultrasound is something like an x-ray. Ultrasound has many uses, one of which is to take a picture of a growing fetus to determine its size and due date.

umbilical cord (um-BILL-ick-uhl cord). The cord that attaches an unborn baby to its mother's uterus. Through the cord, the embryo receives nourishment from the mother.

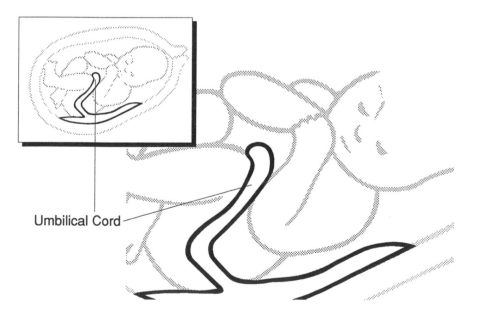

Umbilical Cord

U

ureter (u-REE-ter). A duct that carries away the urine from the kidney to the bladder.

urethra (u-REE-thra). The tube through which urine passes from the bladder during urination. In a male, sperm also is ejaculated through the urethra. See sex organs.

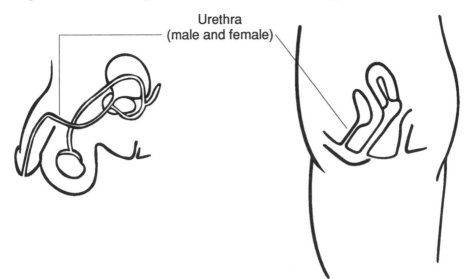

Urethra
(male and female)

urinary infections. One of several infections of the urinary tract that cause painful urination.

uterine contractions. See contractions.

uterine device. See IUD.

U

uterus (U-ter-us)—also called womb. The organ in which a fertilized egg cell develops into a baby. See sex organs.

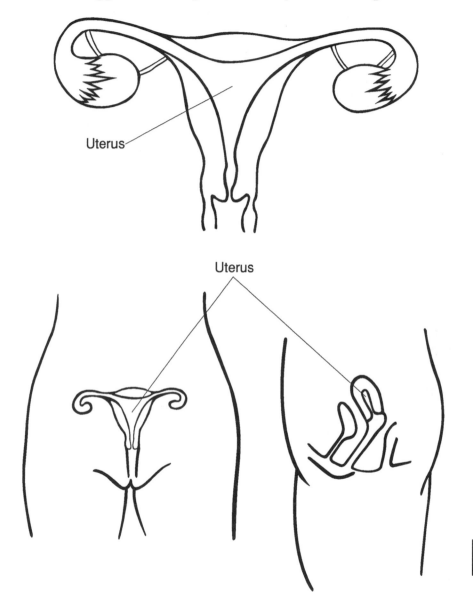

Uterus

Uterus

U

V

vagina (vah-JYE-nah). The passageway leading from the uterus to the outside of a woman's body. The man's penis is inserted into the vagina during intercourse and a baby is normally born through the vagina, if conception occurs. See sex organs.

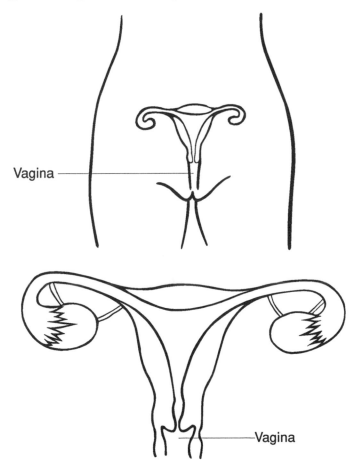

Vagina

Vagina

V

vaginal (VAH-gin-al) **fluids**. Fluids produced in the vagina.

vas deferens (vas DEF-er-enz). One of a pair of tubes through which sperm cells pass from the testicles. See sex organs.

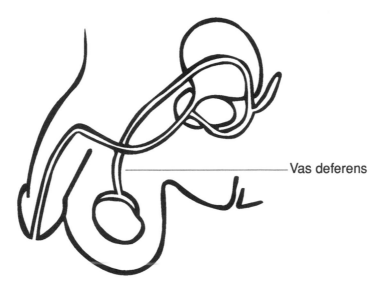

Vas deferens

vasectomy (vas-ECK-tuh-mee). A surgical procedure that prevents sperm from moving through the vas deferens—a method of sterilization.

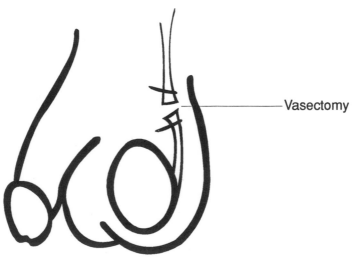

Vasectomy

venereal disease (VD) (vuh-NEER-ee-uhl). See sexually-transmitted disease.

vestibule (VES-teh-bule). In a female, the space between the labia minora into which the vagina and urethra open. See sex organs.

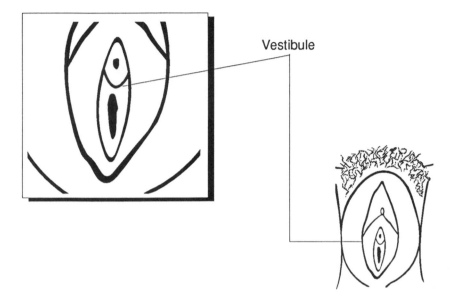

Vestibule

viable (VI-uh-bul). Able to live and develop normally. Usually refers to a baby that is able to live and grow outside the uterus.

virgin (VUR-jun). A person (male or female) who has not had sexual intercourse.

virtue, virtuous. Conforming to high principles. Often refers to being chaste or not having sexual intercourse before marriage.

voice changes. The lowering of a boy's voice common during adolescence.

vulva (VULL-vah). The external area of the female sexual organs that includes the labia and the clitoris. See sex organs.

V

W

wet dream. See nocturnal emission.

withdrawal. A method of birth control where the man's penis is removed from the woman's vagina, before ejaculation of sperm, to prevent pregnancy. Pregnancy, however, sometimes may still occur because semen is present. See also coitus interruptus.

womb (woom). See uterus.

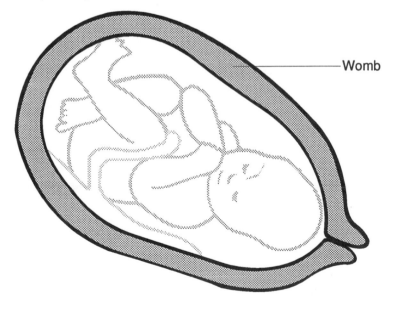

Womb

Y

yeast infection. One of a number of infections that cause itching and burning in the vagina.

Z

zits. Another name for pimples.

zygote (ZI-goat). A fertilized egg cell.

Y
Z

All the Same #1

❖

All five words below begin with the same *first two* letters.

Read the definitions, then fill in the words.

Spanish for male

— — — — —

Hymen

— — — — — — — — — —

Boy or man

— — — —

Legal union of a husband and wife

— — — — — — — —

Physical union of a man and a woman

— — — — — —

See Solutions & Answers — Page 109

All the Same #2

❖

All five words below begin with the same first letter.
Read the definitions, then fill in the words.

Pimples on the face

— — — —

Acquired Immune Deficiency Syndrome

— — — —

Removal of an unborn fetus

— — — — — — — —

Time of life when a girl changes into a young woman
and a boy changes into a young man

— — — — — — — — — —

Part of the body which houses the stomach, the intestines and, in a woman, the uterus or womb

— — — — — — —

See Solutions & Answers — Page 109

10 Letters

❖

Cross out 10 letters below, and what do you have left?

CLUE: The word has to do with having a baby.

P A Z L T E A K M B S Z O B R

20 Letters

❖

Cross out 20 letters below, and what do you have left?

CLUE: A baby normally travels through this.

T E B C K I R R A T F H K M P

Q Z C O R A P B R N M C A E L

See Solutions & Answers — Page 109

Try 'N Find #1

❖

Look for the following 12 human reproduction words:

DIFFERENTIATION, HEREDITY, SEX, MATE, CHROMOSOME, ZYGOTE, INSTINCT, SEMEN, GENDER, GENES, GENETICS, FERTILE

I	N	S	T	I	N	C	T	U	C	P	G	E	N	E	S	D	H	O	U
S	F	G	E	B	L	C	O	T	H	D	E	Z	Q	L	U	A	K	A	C
U	Z	A	L	D	I	F	F	E	R	E	N	T	I	A	T	I	O	N	A
F	E	R	T	I	L	E	H	C	O	L	D	P	O	C	O	H	A	W	K
H	A	C	A	W	E	Z	A	D	M	F	E	Z	W	L	A	C	K	E	I
H	E	R	E	D	I	T	Y	E	O	U	R	D	I	S	E	X	P	E	Z
W	U	Z	E	K	Q	A	T	G	S	E	K	O	U	E	C	O	H	I	T
P	A	T	Z	O	D	D	O	Q	O	L	E	I	D	S	E	M	E	N	D
D	A	C	H	E	C	U	I	F	M	T	A	W	A	Q	I	H	T	E	U
M	S	J	M	A	L	A	O	G	E	N	E	T	I	C	S	E	H	O	D

See Solutions & Answers — Page 109

Try 'N Find #2

❖

Look for the following body parts:
ABDOMEN, BELLY, BLADDER, BOSOM, BREASTS, PELVIS, TESTICLES, URETHRA, UTERUS, WOMB

M	C	A	T	Y	J	O	P	A	N	A	N	I	L	L	E	D	E	M
U	L	E	A	Z	U	T	E	R	U	S	I	T	E	W	A	N	K	E
R	R	W	L	O	E	J	L	I	X	F	A	B	D	O	M	E	N	I
N	O	E	E	T	A	U	A	K	N	O	S	A	M	O	L	A	T	T
I	K	A	T	L	T	O	I	Y	E	M	E	T	I	B	O	A	J	A
H	N	S	C	H	C	I	S	O	A	M	U	R	F	L	O	C	O	K
P	O	E	L	S	R	H	L	U	B	I	I	B	R	E	A	S	T	S
E	M	L	A	B	L	A	D	D	E	R	D	T	A	O	F	F	O	U
R	M	D	I	O	R	C	H	E	L	B	O	E	L	A	N	I	A	M
E	A	U	T	E	S	T	I	C	L	E	S	K	M	U	J	U	Z	Y
S	E	C	I	U	R	E	S	A	Y	O	E	D	I	U	F	R	A	N

See Solutions & Answers — Page 110

Crossword Puzzle #1

❖

1	2	3	4	5	6	7	8	9	10	11	12	13
14		15			16					17		18
19		20	21	22	23	24	25			26		27
28		29			30							31
32							33		34		35
36	37	38	39	40	41	42	43	44	45	46	47	
	48							49		50		
	51	52	53	54	55			56	57	58	59	60
	61						62		63			
64	65	66	67	68				69		70		
	71					72	73	74	75	76		
									77			

ACROSS

1. Joining of a sperm and egg cell
20. Basin-shaped structure in the body
36. Mating and giving birth to children
51. Process of bringing a baby into the world
56. Sexual arousal of a male by a female in heat—usually in animals
64. Maidenhead
72. Tiny units of heredity

DOWN

1. Male who brings offspring into the world
3. Forced intercourse
6. Caring deeply for someone
11. Intrauterine device
13. Bellybutton
33. Unable to have children
34. Soft spot in a baby's head
37. Unborn baby

See Solutions & Answers — Page 110

Crossword Puzzle #2

❖

ACROSS

1. Science of heredity
10. Pimples or zits
21. Fringes at end of fallopian tubes
33. Part of a cell nucleus
50. Contractions during childbirth
62. Fertile time in female cycle
66. Male
76. Sexually-transmitted disease
81. Every person has one
86. Type of contraceptive
91. Unborn child
99. Keeping the body clean
110. Premature baby
117. A tiny baby

DOWN

1. Homosexual
8. Male or female
9. Complicated process used by the reproductive cells
13. Incision used at childbirth
19. Uterus
24. Mammary gland
28. Tube through which urine passes
33. Intercourse
40. Egg cell
78. Cleansing solution
90. Maidenhead

See Solutions & Answers — Page 111

What's the Story?
Fill in the Missing Vowels

❖

A Baby is Born

S_lly w_k_n_d h_r h_sb_nd _t 3:00 _.m. Sh_ w_s h_v_ng c_ntr_ct__ns, _nd sh_ f_lt _t w_s t_m_ t_ g_ t_ th_ h_sp_t_l. H_r _bst_tr_c__n w_s w__t_ng f_r th_m wh_n th_y _rr_v_d.

Th_ d_ct_r _x_m_n_d S_lly _nd s__d th_ b_by w__ld s__n b_ _n th_ b_rth c_n_l, b_t th_t _t w_s br__ch. H_ t_ld S_lly sh_ m_ght n__d t_ h_v_ _ c_s_r__n s_ct__n.

Th_ b_by h_d b__n gr_w_ng _n S_lly's _t_r_s f_r th_ p_st n_n_ m_nths. N_w w_s th_ b_g m_m_nt. S_lly's l_b_r p__ns w_r_ b_c_m_ng m_r_ _nt_ns_. Th_s w_s d_f_n_t_ly n_t f_ls_ l_b_r.

_t w_s thr_ll_ng f_r S_lly _nd J_m t_ r__l_z_ th_t _ t_ny sp_rm c_ll h_d f_rt_l_z_d _ t_ny _gg c_ll m_ny m_nths _g_. Fr_m th_s _n__n _n _mbry_ h_d b_g_n t_ gr_w. Th_t _mbry_ h_d n_w d_v_l_p_d _nt_ _ n_w b_by r__dy t_ b_ b_rn.

Th_ d_ct_r w_s _bl_ t_ t_rn th_ b_by s_ th_t S_lly c__ld h_v_ _ n_t_r_l ch_ldb_rth. B_f_r_ l_ng S_lly _nd J_m w_r_ th_ pr__d p_r_nts _f _ b__t_f_l b_by g_rl.

See Solutions & Answers — Page 112

What's the Story?
Fill in the Missing Vowels
❖

Growing Up Is Fun

B_ng_t_n g_r_s_n_xc_t_ngt_m_. _s__rly_s_g_
__ght, s_m_ g_rls b_g_n th_ pr_c_ss _f _d_l_sc_nc_.
_n_th_r_n_m_ f_r _d_l_sc_nc_ _s p_b_rty.
  Th_s _s th_ t_m_ wh_n g_rls b_g_n t_ ch_ng_ _nt_
y__ng w_m_n _nd b_ys b_g_n t_ ch_ng_ _nt_ y__ng
m_n. G_rls, h_w_v_r, _lm_st _lw_ys d_v_l_p f_st_r th_n
b_ys. L_t_r _n, b_ys gr_w phys_c_lly f_st_r th_n g_rls.
  Th_ p_t__t_ry gl_nd _n th_ br__n st_rts th_ pr_c_ss.
_v_ry b_y _nd g_rl d_v_l_ps _t _ d_ff_r_nt r_t_.
  _n_ ch_ng_ m_st g_rls _nd b_ys _xp_r__nc_ _s _cn_.
_n_th_r_n_m_ f_r _cn_ _s p_mpl_s _r z_ts. Th_s _s
th__ght t_ b_ c__s_d by _v_r_ct_v_ s_b_c___s gl_nds _n
th_ sk_n. _cn_ _sn't f_n, b_t _t d__sn't l_st f_r_v_r.
  _n _xc_t_ng p_rt _f gr_w_ng _p _s d_t_ng _nd sh_r_ng
g__d t_m_s w_th fr__nds. _t's _ls_ _ n_t_r_l _k f_rw_rd t_
b_c_m_ng _n _d_lt _nd _n _d_y m_rry_ng _nd h_v_ng _
f_m_ly.

See Solutions & Answers — Page 113

Word Search #1

❖

See if you can find eight words dealing with dating days:

ACNE, ADOLESCENCE, DATING, EMOTIONS, KISS, PIMPLES, PUBERTY, ZITS

P	A	N	G	R	O	M	X	E	O	R	I	V	E	L
E	P	I	M	P	L	E	S	H	L	A	K	U	M	A
L	O	U	D	H	E	T	A	F	I	C	A	I	O	P
V	I	R	B	A	L	X	G	L	A	N	H	I	T	E
A	D	O	L	E	S	C	E	N	C	E	L	F	I	T
X	A	V	E	P	R	A	I	G	E	V	E	A	O	K
G	L	O	Z	Z	I	T	S	H	D	A	T	I	N	G
K	I	S	S	A	P	E	Y	U	N	G	I	L	S	T

See Solutions & Answers — Page 114

Word Search #2

❖

Look for the following sexually-transmitted disease words:

CHLAMYDIA, TRICHOMONAS, CRABS, DISEASE,
GONORRHEA, GONOCOCCUS, CHANCRE, HERPES, AIDS

C	E	S	T	R	I	C	H	O	M	O	N	A	S	J	O	Y	I
H	S	U	R	O	X	I	S	A	S	U	O	H	Y	R	A	Z	R
L	A	B	E	A	G	O	R	E	Y	Q	A	O	Q	B	S	E	U
A	O	J	Q	U	I	O	O	N	O	L	R	X	E	B	S	Q	U
M	R	E	O	J	G	O	N	O	R	R	H	E	A	R	I	Y	J
Y	S	A	B	O	J	R	X	O	B	I	Q	R	U	I	E	D	O
D	I	S	E	A	S	E	Q	X	C	U	C	A	K	O	D	U	H
I	U	E	S	B	Q	U	E	R	U	O	H	E	R	P	E	S	A
A	O	U	O	Z	A	I	Y	J	E	Y	C	Z	L	J	O	A	L
Q	L	A	H	B	L	O	Q	C	H	A	N	C	R	E	S	R	B
S	I	R	X	S	A	S	R	T	O	W	F	E	U	R	Y	X	O
A	K	S	E	P	U	T	A	Q	W	E	R	K	H	S	Z	U	E

See Solutions & Answers — Page 114

Know Your Words #1

❖

Circle the correct letter

1. An unborn baby is called a:

   A. fimbria
   B. sebum
   C. fetus

2. A doctor who delivers babies is:

   A. an obstetrician
   B. a vasectomy
   C. a heterosexual

3. An IUD is:

   A. a newborn baby
   B. the menstrual cycle
   C. a birth control device

4. Not being able to have children means being:

   A. impotent
   B. nauseated
   C. bisexual

5. A baby born before nine months is a:

   A. Lamaze baby
   B. premature baby
   C. Wasserman baby

6. "Change of life" is another term for:

   A. puberty
   B. dating years
   C. menopause

7. Breast feeding is also called:

   A. nursing
   B. copulation
   C. necking

8. Fontanel is another name for a baby's:

   A. bladder
   B. "soft spot"
   C. abdomen

9. The gland that begins the body changes at adolescence is the:

   A. prostate gland
   B. mammary gland
   C. pituitary gland

10. Puberty is another name for:

   A. adolescence
   B. quickening
   C. AIDS

11. An operation that prevents a person from having children is:

   A. zygote
   B. sterilization
   C. syphilis

12. When a baby is born buttocks first, it is a:

   A. breech birth
   B. cesarean section
   C. circumcision

13. This is what is removed during circumcision:

   A. Adam's apple
   B. nipple
   C. foreskin

14. A female homosexual is a:

   A. molester
   B. lesbian
   C. virgin

15. Keeping the body clean and healthy is:

   A. hygiene
   B. labor
   C. gender identity

16. When a sperm cell and an egg cell join, this is what takes place:

   A. abstinence
   B. conception
   C. birth control

See Solutions & Answers — Page 115

Know Your Words #2

❖

Circle the correct letter

1. chromosome:

   A. a common disease
   B. cell nucleus containing DNA
   C. a surgical instrument
   D. an unborn child

2. coitus

   A. sexual intercourse
   B. part of the abdomen
   C. hygiene method
   D. an emotion

3. differentiation

   A. navel
   B. a complicated process of fetal development
   C. fertilization
   D. the velvety lining of the uterus

4. fertile

   A. change of life
   B. able to have children
   C. breech birth
   D. bosom

5. gender

   A. being either male or female
   B. crabs
   C. basal body temperature method
   D. amniocentesis

6. genes

   A. estrogen
   B. diaphragm
   C. fetal alcohol syndrome
   D. units of heredity

7. genetics

   A. endometrium
   B. science of heredity
   C. natural childbirth
   D. reproductive organs

8. herpes

   A. a flu germ
   B. viral disease of the skin
   C. a growth spurt
   D. small bugs

9. heredity

A. characteristics passed through the genes
B. nausea
C. placenta
D. premarital intercourse

10. heterosexual

A. a person attracted to someone of the same sex
B. illegitimate child
C. sexually transmitted disease
D. a person attracted to someone of the opposite sex

11. hormones

A. zits
B. chemicals secreted by the glands
C. urinary infections
D. membranes in the body

12. instinct

A. sterility
B. viable
C. natural impulse
D. fimbria

13. mate

A. intercourse
B. gestation
C. abstinence
D. cervix

14. menopause

A. men who pause or stop
B. hymen
C. "change of life"
D. sex change

15. midwife

A. more than one wife
B. someone who delivers a baby
C. a hospital orderly
D. a child caretaker

16. navel

A. bellybutton
B. sailor
C. newborn baby
D. moral

17. offspring

A. a broken spring
B. egg cell
C. nursing
D. children

18. semen

    A. part of the bladder
    B. gender
    C. estrogen
    D. fluid containing sperm

19. sex

    A. zygote
    B. male or female
    C. epididymis
    D. sterility

20. zygote

    A. fontanel
    B. fraternal twin
    C. fertilized egg cell
    D. Adam's apple

See Solutions & Answers — Page 115

Solutions & Answers

Answers to All the Same #1 (page 93):
1. Macho
2. Maidenhead
3. Male
4. Marriage
5. Mating

Answers to All the Same #2 (page 94):
1. Acne
2. AIDS
3. Abortion
4. Adolescence
5. Abdomen

Answer to 10 Letters (page 95): LABOR

Answer to 20 Letters (page 95): BIRTH CANAL

Solution to Try 'N Find #1 (page 96):

I	N	S	T	I	N	C	T	U	C	P	G	E	N	E	S	O	H	O	U
S	F	G	E	B	L	C	O	T	H	O	E	Z	O	L	U	R	K	R	C
U	Z	R	L	D	I	F	F	E	R	E	N	T	I	A	T	I	O	N	R
F	E	R	T	I	L	E	H	C	O	L	D	P	O	C	O	H	R	U	K
H	R	C	R	U	E	Z	R	O	M	F	E	Z	U	L	R	C	K	E	I
H	E	R	E	D	I	T	Y	C	O	U	R	O	I	S	E	H	P	E	Z
U	U	Z	E	K	O	R	T	G	S	C	K	O	U	C	O	H	I	I	T
P	R	T	Z	O	O	O	O	O	O	L	E	I	B	S	E	M	E	N	O
O	A	C	H	E	C	U	I	F	M	T	R	U	R	O	I	H	T	C	U
M	S	J	M	R	L	B	O	G	E	N	E	T	I	C	S	C	H	O	B

Solution to Try 'N Find #2 (page 97):

M	C	A	T	Y	J	O	P	R	N	A	N	I	L	L	E	O	E	M
U	L	E	A	Z	U	T	E	R	U	S	I	T	E	W	A	N	K	E
A	R	W	L	O	E	J	L	I	K	F	A	B	D	O	M	E	N	I
N	O	E	I	T	A	D	V	A	K	N	O	S	A	M	O	L	A	T
I	K	A	T	L	T	O	I	Y	E	M	E	T	I	B	O	A	J	A
H	N	S	C	H	C	I	S	O	A	M	U	A	F	L	O	C	O	K
P	O	E	L	S	R	H	L	U	B	I	I	B	R	E	A	S	T	S
E	M	L	A	B	L	A	D	D	E	R	D	T	A	O	F	F	O	U
R	M	O	I	O	A	C	A	E	L	B	O	E	L	A	N	I	A	M
E	A	U	T	E	S	T	I	C	L	E	S	K	M	U	J	U	Z	Y
S	E	C	I	V	A	E	S	A	Y	O	E	O	I	V	F	R	A	N

Solution to Crossword Puzzle #1 (page 98):

1 F	2 E	3 R	4 T	5 I	6 L	7 I	8 Z	9 A	10 T	11 I	12 O	13 N
14 A		15 A			16 O					17 U		18 A
19 T		20 P	21 E	22 L	23 U	24 I	25 S			26 D		27 U
28 H		29 E		30 E								31 E
32 E							33 S		34 F		35 L	
36 R	37 E	38 P	39 R	40 O	41 D	42 U	43 C	44 T	45 I	46 O	47 N	
	48 M						49 E		50 N			
	51 B	52 I	53 R	54 T	55 H		56 R	57 U	58 T	59 T	60 Y	
	61 R						62 I		63 A			
64 H	65 Y	66 M	67 E	68 N			69 L		70 N			
	71 O					72 G	73 E	74 N	75 E	76 S		
									77 L			

Solution to Crossword Puzzle #2 (page 99):

¹G	²E	³N	⁴E	⁵T	⁶I	⁷C	⁸S		⁹D		¹⁰A	¹¹C	¹²N ¹³E
¹⁴A							¹⁵E	¹⁶I					¹⁷P
¹⁸Y			¹⁹W		²⁰K		²¹F	²²I	²³M	²⁴B	²⁵R	²⁶I	²⁷A
	²⁸U		²⁹O			³⁰F		³¹R			³²S		
³³C	³⁴H	³⁵R	³⁶O	³⁷M	³⁸O	³⁹S	⁴⁰O	⁴¹M	⁴²E		⁴³E		⁴⁴I
⁴⁵O		⁴⁶E		⁴⁷B			⁴⁸U	⁴⁹R		⁵⁰L	⁵¹A	⁵²B	⁵³O ⁵⁴R
⁵⁵I		⁵⁶T				⁵⁷U		⁵⁸E			⁵⁹S		⁶⁰T
⁶¹T		⁶²H	⁶³E	⁶⁴A	⁶⁵T	⁶⁶M	⁶⁷A	⁶⁸N			⁶⁹T		⁷⁰O
⁷¹U		⁷²R					⁷³T						⁷⁴M
⁷⁵S		⁷⁶A	⁷⁷I	⁷⁸D	⁷⁹S			⁸⁰I		⁸¹B	⁸²O	⁸³D	⁸⁴Y
			⁸⁵O		⁸⁶F	⁸⁷O	⁸⁸A	⁸⁹M					⁹⁰H
	⁹¹F	⁹²E	⁹³T	⁹⁴U	⁹⁵S			⁹⁶T					⁹⁷Y
			⁹⁸C		⁹⁹H	¹⁰⁰Y	¹⁰¹G	¹⁰²I	¹⁰³E	¹⁰⁴N	¹⁰⁵E		¹⁰⁶M
			¹⁰⁷H					¹⁰⁸D					¹⁰⁹E
¹¹⁰P	¹¹¹R	¹¹²E	¹¹³E	¹¹⁴M	¹¹⁵I	¹¹⁶E		¹¹⁷N	¹¹⁸E	¹¹⁹W	¹²⁰B	¹²¹O	¹²²R ¹²³N

What's the Story?
(page 100)
Solution

A Baby is Born

Sally wakened her husband at 3:00 a.m. She was having contractions, and she felt it was time to go to the hospital. Her obstetrician was waiting for them when they arrived.

The doctor examined Sally and said the baby would soon be in the birth canal, but that it was breech. He told Sally she might need to have a cesarean section.

The baby had been growing in Sally's uterus for the past nine months. Now was the big moment. Sally's labor pains were becoming more intense. This was definitely not false labor.

It was thrilling for Sally and Jim to realize that a tiny sperm cell had fertilized a tiny egg cell many months ago. From this union an embryo had begun to grow. That embryo had now developed into a new baby ready to be born.

The doctor was able to turn the baby so that Sally could have natural childbirth. Before long Sally and Jim were the proud parents of a beautiful baby girl.

What's the Story?
(page 101)
Solution

Growing Up Is Fun

Being a teenager is an exciting time. As early as age eight, some girls begin the process of adolescence. Another name for adolescence is puberty.

This is the time when girls begin to change into young women and boys begin to change into young men. Girls, however, almost always develop faster than boys. Later on, boys grow physically faster than girls.

The pituitary gland in the brain starts the process. Every boy and girl develops at a different rate.

One change most girls and boys experience is acne. Another name for acne is pimples or zits. This is thought to be caused by overactive sebaceous glands in the skin. Acne isn't fun, but it doesn't last forever.

An exciting part of growing up is dating and sharing good times with friends. It's also fun to look forward to becoming an adult and one day marrying and having a family.

P	R	N	G	R	O	M	K	E	O	R	I	D	E	L
E	P	I	M	P	L	E	S	H	L	A	K	U	M	R
L	O	U	O	H	E	T	R	F	I	C	R	I	O	P
U	J	R	B	R	L	K	G	L	R	N	K	I	T	E
A	D	O	L	E	S	C	E	N	C	E	L	F	I	T
K	R	U	E	P	R	R	J	G	E	U	E	R	O	K
G	L	O	Z	Z	I	T	S	H	D	A	T	I	N	G
K	I	S	S	R	P	E	Y	U	N	G	J	L	S	T

C	E	S	T	R	I	C	H	O	M	O	N	A	S	J	O	Y	I
H	S	U	R	O	H	J	S	R	S	D	O	H	Y	R	R	Z	R
L	R	O	E	R	G	O	R	E	Y	Q	R	O	Q	R	S	E	U
A	O	J	O	D	I	O	O	N	O	L	R	H	E	B	S	Q	D
M	R	E	O	J	G	O	N	O	R	R	H	E	R	R	J	Y	J
Y	S	R	R	O	J	R	H	O	R	J	Q	R	U	I	E	R	O
D	I	S	E	A	S	E	Q	H	C	U	C	R	K	O	D	U	H
I	D	E	S	R	Q	D	E	R	D	O	H	E	R	P	E	S	R
A	O	D	O	Z	R	J	Y	J	E	Y	C	Z	L	J	O	R	L
Q	L	R	H	R	L	O	Q	C	H	A	N	C	R	E	S	R	R
S	J	R	R	S	R	S	R	T	O	W	F	E	U	R	Y	R	O
R	K	S	E	P	D	T	R	Q	W	E	R	K	H	S	Z	D	E

Answers to Know Your Words #1 (page 104):

1. — C
2. — A
3. — C
4. — A
5. — B
6. — C
7. — A
8. — B

9. — C
10. — A
11. — B
12. — A
13. — C
14. — B
15. — A
16. — B

Answers to Know Your Words #2 (page 106):

1. — B
2. — A
3. — B
4. — B
5. — A
6. — D
7. — B
8. — C
9. — A
10. — D

11. — B
12. — C
13. — A
14. — C
15. — B
16. — A
17. — D
18. — D
19. — B
20. — C

About the Authors

❖

Dean and Nancy Hoch are the parents of five children. They are native Pennsylvanians who moved to Idaho after living in California for a number of years. Both are active in school and community organizations.

Dean Hoch holds a doctorate in education from the University of California at Berkeley. He has been a teacher, principal, and college professor. Nancy Hoch's background is in Training and Development through Idaho State University. Together, they have established and operated several successful small businesses.

The Hochs share a combined experience of over twenty years in education, counseling, and youth leadership. They are concerned about the welfare of young people.

Members of the ASJA (American Society of Journalists and Authors), they have written two other books as well as articles for some 35-40 national magazines. Their magazine credits include *Reader's Digest, Good Housekeeping, Boys' Life,* and many more.

Their other books are titled *Go for the Eagle, a Guide to Achieving Scouting's Highest Honor,* and *Boy, oh, Boy: Boy-Raising Secrets Every Parent Should Know.*

They co-author nearly everything they write, and this book is no exception. They have recently formed a publishing company of their own, and this is the second book they have produced.